Climb Aboard

For Dreamers and Visionaries

Based on a True Story

This book is dedicated to dreamers and visionaries.

Climb Aboard

For Dreamers and Visionaries

By Susan Huppert
Illustrated by Rachel White

Homegrown Publications, LLC • Red Wing, MN

Text copyright © 2009 by Susan Huppert
Illustrations copyright © 2009 by Rachel White

Scripture taken from the HOLY BIBLE, NEW INTERNATIONAL VERSION®. NIV®. Copyright© 1973, 1978, 1984 by International Bible Society. Used by permission of Zondervan. All rights reserved.

No part of this book may be reproduced, stored in a retrieval system, or transmitted in any form or by any means, electronic, mechanical, photocopying, recording, or otherwise without written permission of Homegrown Publications, LLC.

Homegrown Publications, P.O. Box 173, Red Wing, MN 55066
Printed in the United States of America

ISBN 978-0-9799635-1-3

Mr. Ross stood at the big glass window of the airport watching another plane crawl to a halt on the runway. The airport was an exciting place to work. The planes were big and loud and fast. Each day new people bustled through the airport on their way to someplace else.

It was Mr. Ross' job to see that the travelers were happy. So, every morning he strolled through the terminal making sure everything was going smoothly. He smiled at the ladies in the coffee shop. He waved to the ticket agents. He always complimented the custodians who kept the airport clean and shiny. He liked his work. But he often dreamed of something else.

Ever since Mr. Ross was a young boy he loved trains. Even now, when he was older and becoming bald, his passion for trains only grew stronger.

Although he lived miles away from any train stations, he booked a ride on a train every chance he had. He planned meetings on trains. He traveled through the mountains on trains. Occasionally Mr. Ross rode a new train route to see the sights. On long trips, he would sleep or eat on the trains and meet new people; like porters or conductors and other travelers. Mr. Ross liked to sit in the dome car and watch the scenery - or just relax and think.

One night, Mr. Ross had a dream that he turned a caboose into an ice cream shop. The dream made him smile in his sleep as children from all over the neighborhood lined up to buy his ice cream.

The next day, when Lorna was baking Woof Wafers for her dogs, her husband told her that he wanted to buy a caboose and turn it into an ice cream shop.
"Turn a caboose into an ice cream shop?!!" exclaimed Lorna. "That's impossible! Where would we find someone with a caboose for sale? How would we move it? Where would we put it? That sounds impossible!"

So Mr. Ross tried to forget the idea. But the idea would not go away. Every weekend he studied the want ads in the Sunday newspaper searching for someone who wanted to sell a caboose. Then, on a beautiful summer day, as he relaxed in his hammock under the big Maple tree in his front yard, Mr. Ross saw an ad in a train magazine that read:

The train magazine flew into the air as Mr. Ross untangled himself from the hammock and ran to the kitchen to tell Lorna. He had found a caboose!

The next day, Lorna and Mr. Ross loaded their lunch and their dogs into their old blue pick-up truck and set off to find the caboose.

After miles and miles of driving, Mr. Ross noticed the faded red caboose he had read about, sitting alone on an embedded train track in the distance. The small caboose was overcome with weeds and tall grasses and its wheels were rusty from age.

Parking his truck, he ran through the tall grass toward the old caboose. It was rickety and needed repair. But in his mind, Sooline Number 27 sparkled like a cherry red apple under the summer sun. He imagined children coming to the caboose for ice cream on hot summer days. He thought about dogs happily romping and eating Woof Wafers in the back yard of the ice cream shop, and travelers from the big city that would stop to see the novelty on their Sunday drives.

"This is the caboose of my dreams," Mr. Ross told his wife. "I'm going to take it home."

Not long after that, a huge semi-truck pulled into Bay City towing an enormous flat bed trailer with the ragged red caboose perched on top. The Lift Me High Crane Company arrived at the location Mr. Ross had selected along the Great River Road.

People gathered from everywhere to watch the rickety little caboose as it lifted off the truck and came to rest on a special train track built for it. Some people applauded and cheered. Others laughed and said, "That will never work."

But the nay-sayers didn't deter Mr. Ross. His determination only grew stronger and stronger.

That night when Mr. Ross went to bed he smiled as he slept. He knew if he worked hard, his dream would become real and Flat Pennies Ice Cream® would serve its community along the mighty Mississippi River for many years to come.

And so it did.

"Climb Aboard," a story of optimism and inspiration captures the challenges of creative thinkers in a delightful story derived from a true experience of Jim and Lorna Ross, owners of Flat Pennies Ice Cream®.

Flat Pennies Ice Cream® began with an interest in trains and a business idea during the winter of 2001 when the couple purchased the SooLine caboose #27. The caboose was temporarily stored at the Colfax Railroad Museum in Colfax, Wisconsin. Once the location for the ice cream shop was located, the caboose was moved to the tiny berg of Bay City, Wisconsin.

An icon of inspiration for future dreamers and visionaries rests along the Great River Road between majestic bluffs and the mighty Mississippi River where it came to rest in 2006.